D1487450

DESPERATE CUPCAKES

HELLO my name is

Betty B. Good

HELLO my name is

MO SUGGAH

Chris

HELLO my name is

ADA SWEETE

HELLO my name is

Lotta Cal O'Reese

HE

Ed

HELLO my name is

Yumi Intumi

HELLO my name is

Coco I. Sing

H

MO

HELLO my name is

HELLO my name is

Bea D. Licious

Eddie Belle

A.

DESPERATE CUPCAKES

By Anita Dyette

Potter Style
NEW YORK

Copyright © 2010 by Potter Style,
a division of Random House, Inc.

All rights reserved.

Published in the United States by Potter Style,
an imprint of the Crown Publishing Group,
a division of Random House, Inc., New York.
www.crownpublishing.com
www.clarksonpotter.com

Potter Style and the Potter Style colophon
are trademarks of Random House, Inc.

Library of Congress Cataloging-in-Publication Data
is available upon request

ISBN 978-0-307-71852-5

Printed in China

Design by Danielle Deschenes
Photographs by Amy Kalyn Sims

10 9 8 7 6 5 4 3 2 1

First Edition

WHAT'S SO DESPERATE ABOUT A CUPCAKE?

If you haven't noticed by now, cupcakes are at the zenith of their popularity. Formerly relegated to kids' birthdays and school-bake sales, these little cakes have achieved the same renown as the once-modest cup of coffee. They've spawned an entire industry of high-priced cafés with lines around the block. They come in every flavor imaginable and are tricked-out in increasingly elaborate decorations. More than a tasty snack, the cupcake has become a vehicle for self-expression, social consciousness, and good taste.

This is precisely why cupcakes are feeling desperate. Listen closely and you'll hear them feverishly asking themselves, "This is all great, but what's next?" Cupcakes don't want to be merely consumed. They want to harness their notoriety and parlay it into something even bigger. As a result, these little desserts have forgotten where they come from, and they don't know where they're going. It's the classic recipe for insecurity.

This photo essay is my attempt to capture the inner world of the contemporary cupcake. Be warned; it's not exactly the sweet, cream-filled place that one assumes it to be, but it should look familiar.

— *Anita Dyette*

CUPCAKE RULES

Cupcakes maintain a world view in which they are socially distinct from other desserts. They aren't exactly certain why they pulled ahead of the pack, but they sure-as-sugar aren't about to cede their place at the top.

Cupcakes do not tolerate muffins. In the eyes of a cupcake, a muffin is a dense, oily, underdressed ruffian who must be shunned at all costs. In truth, cupcakes have an intense fear that muffins might overtake them in popularity. It's a paranoid and uncharitable way of thinking, but this is how success warps the mind.

Cupcakes basically feel sorry for big ol'-fashioned cakes. People care about variety, individuality, and portion control these days, and traditionally sized cakes are just missing the boat on all counts. Who wants to be cut up into little pieces and frozen for later? Gross.

Cookies aren't particularly threatening. Their ranks are too diverse to mobilize the kind of PR campaign needed to overtake cupcakes. Some are totally nuts and others only come out during the holidays. Cupcakes are keeping close tabs on the cream-filled sandwich and glazed varieties. Any dessert that dabbles in frosting is asking for trouble.

Pies are not cute. They look nice for about two seconds, but by the end of the evening they're a sloppy mess. Tarts try harder—perhaps too hard—to be liked, but their crusty disposition can be off-putting.

Jell-o is a salad. It is not a dessert. It doesn't count.

Being Cute Is a Crap Shoot

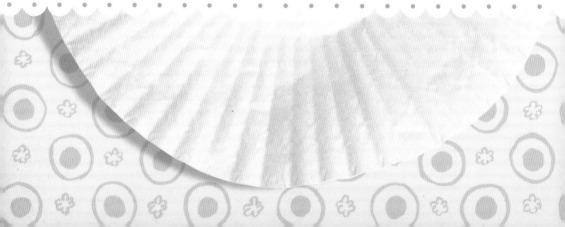

Nobody has time for a sloppily made cupcake these days. Hence almost every cupcake worries about staying in shape. They tinker with the color of their frosting, overcompensate with fancy decorations, and suffer embarrassing mishaps in an effort to maintain a rigorous standard of cuteness. It takes more than a tough cookie to endure this kind of pressure.

Though her yoga gear was sweet, Buttercup's side-plank pose was nothing to write ohm about.

"Crepes!" exclaimed Colette as she stepped on the bathroom scale. The time for excuses was over: she had to start working on her muffin top.

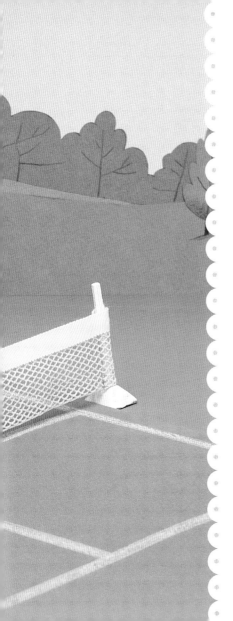

Wendy didn't need a partner.
After three clubhouse martinis,
she was already seeing doubles.

Having recently moved from New Jersey,
Bianca wasn't yet familiar with country casual.

Fifi's friends assured her the new color would
look totally different in natural light.

‹ Back to Messages | Mark as Unread | Report Spam | Delete

 Darla April 5 at 4:26pm
OMG. 2 blu 2 B 4-gotten!

 Monique April 5 at 4:28pm
ROFL. Nothing compares 2 Blu!

 Darla April 5 at 4:29pm
LOL. 2 BLU 4 ME & U.

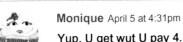 **Monique** April 5 at 4:31pm
Yup, U get wut U pay 4.

Darla April 5 at 4:32pm
4 sure! Glad I spent $$$$ on my frosting 2day.

 Monique April 5 at 4:35pm
ROFLMAO. Thatz wut haps when U go 4 the blu-plate "special"!

She tried a racer-back, two one-pieces,
and three bikinis, but Betty still
couldn't find anything in her cup size.

The other club members screamed for her
to come down, but Betty didn't listen. Having
tried on sixty-seven ill-fitting swimsuits,
she was ready to go off the deep end.

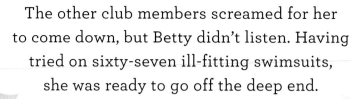

Lovin' from the Oven

Back in simpler times, cupcakes didn't stray far from their own batch. Now cupcakes want passion, romance, and adventure, but they don't want to sacrifice security, familiarity, and their wholesome image. As a result, more than one cupcake will wake up at 3:00 a.m. in a sudden panic: Was it unwise to refuse a second date with my tax accountant? Who is this old coot sleeping next to me? And whatever happened to that spring break sex tape? Yes, life is tricky when you try to have your cake and eat it, too.

Sure, Sid was from the wrong side of the cooling rack,
but Sunshine couldn't resist that devil's food.

No doubt about it,
their relationship was messy.

Samantha was resourceful. When her parents stopped paying off her credit card debt, she found herself a sugar daddy.

"He's too vanilla for my taste," thought Celeste. "But this beats another Friday night in front of the TV, dining on Hot Pockets and chardonnay."

Maybe she wasn't as young and fresh as the other hostesses, but Sally knew how to deal with this bunch of ding-dongs.

The discovery was too much to bear: Delilah's stud was really a muffin.

Janice wanted more sizzle in the bedroom.
But when Milton brought home the bacon,
this wasn't what he had in mind.

Claudia was starting to wonder about Vlad. They only went out at night. He always looked hungry, but refused to share her popcorn. And his online dating profile expressed a specific preference for red velvet cupcakes. It didn't make any bloody sense.

Stella picked the wrong night to
serve herself on a silver platter.
The L.A. Cakers were in the bakeoffs.

When Jarvis left her for a young gold-digger, Maude moved to Florida and met a lifeguard.

SUGAR LIPS

HONEY BUNS

After ditching her groom, Delilah quickly found comfort in Brad, who had been dumped by Stella. Well, at least he's not a muffin!

Linda and Elron hooked up in Vegas. Unfortunately, she brought home a souvenir.

SUGAR LIPS + HONEY BUNS

HONEY BUNS

Yolanda is looking for the next flavor of the month.

When things didn't work out with the punk, Sunshine had the good sense to move on to a stoner.

They go to the same bars, but it's nothing serious.

Motherhood

Few cupcakes can resist their hardwired sense of responsibility to bring more adorableness to the planet. Given their incredible popularity, the pressure to find a toothsome mate and produce a cute little baby cake is stronger than ever. However, once this basic task is achieved, all bets are off. Each mother must decide for herself how to raise a good cake, and we all know there's no easy recipe for that.

When Everyone Wants a Piece of You

Amy had eight kids and another one in the oven. It was enough reality for anyone. So where was her TV contract?

Linda sped to the ladies room for the third time that morning. "Morning sickness?" Joan asked slyly, assessing Linda's pale green pallor. "Not at all," Linda denied, swallowing hard. "This is pistachio frosting."

When the police questioned him later in life, Dexter would cite "the leash" as his evil turning point. "Never mind the beanie or our matching outfits," he explained. "She shackled me to her side like a lowly pupcake."

Matt would never forget the
mortifying day Mom discovered his
enormous cupcake porn stash.

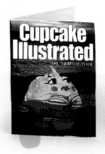

There was no way that Peggy was going
to let the triplets go trick-or-treating
dressed like a bunch of tarts.

Crumby Kids

Cupcake children can be a bit fresh, to say the least. Many take their favored place in the pantheon of desserts very much for granted and therefore don't try very hard to be sweet. But, really, how many times a day can you hear "You're skating on thin icing, young lady" and take it seriously? Young cupcakes aren't willing to walk on eggshells, and, in a way, you have to admire their moxie.

"Oopsie!" giggled Mary Agnes when her dodge
ball hit Mary Catherine right in her sweet spot.

Jonah could tell that Kimmy's first day in Berkeley was off to a rocky start. Everyone here was vegan or gluten-free and wore recycled wrappers. It was no place for an O.C. girl with a refined-sugar background.

It was 4:20 p.m.—time to get baked.

The jams flew fast and furious at Wrapper's Delight, the third annual Cupcake City hip-hop convention. Could Vanilla Icing finally outflow Cake Mix Master Mike?

The dance competition was going well for the cupcakes, until Melvin attempted an ill-advised headspin. Five minutes later, his teammates were scraping him off the floor.

The girls knew they shouldn't take candy
from strangers, but Lily had a plan.
"Never mind his Jujubes," she snapped at
her sisters, "get the chocolate bars and run!"

When Bad Things

Cupcakes are tasty. They are also perishable. One way or another, each little cake is going to have to make an appointment with that big pie-maker in the sky. This is not an easy thing to accept. In a twisted attempt to take control of fate, some cupcakes exhibit an appetite for self-destruction. In extreme cases, they will even turn against each other. One thing a cupcake absolutely will not do, however, is feast on its own kind.

Happen to Baked Goods

Ever since joining the Hell's Angel Food Cakes,
Elron thought he was invincible.

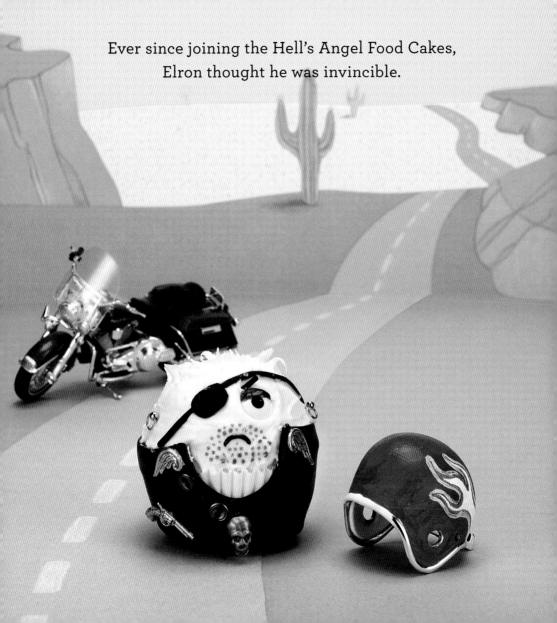

Dr. Bob hadn't seen a sugar crash
this bad in a long time.

Brooke and her friends decided
to skip the appetizers.

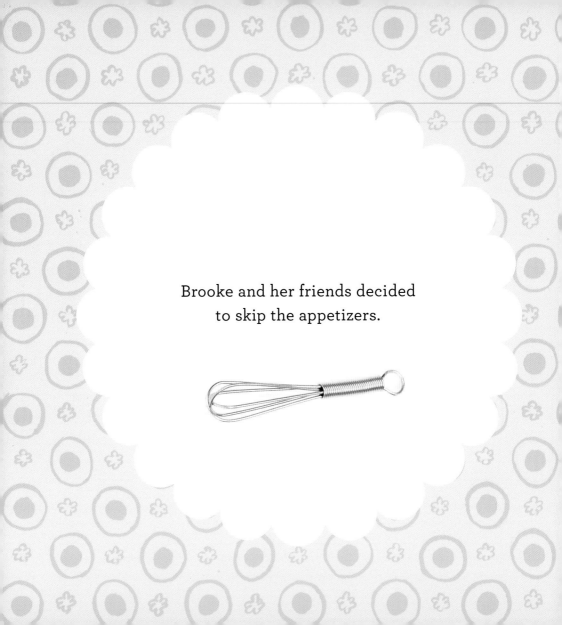

All of Joe's favorite books and movies had been predicting a zombie outbreak for years. Yet here he was, without a toothpick in sight.

" 'Let them eat cake' sounds so much nicer than 'Bite me,' "
thought Marie. "I hope the peasants get my joke."

Working nine to five was getting stale. When Candy's boss nicknamed her Coffee Cake, she began envisioning revenge scenarios.

CALORIES: 3978
FAT: 97 g

It looked like Minerva and Harold were going to ace the cupcake self-defense class; no one would reach for such harmful foods. Bart, on the other hand, was in trouble.

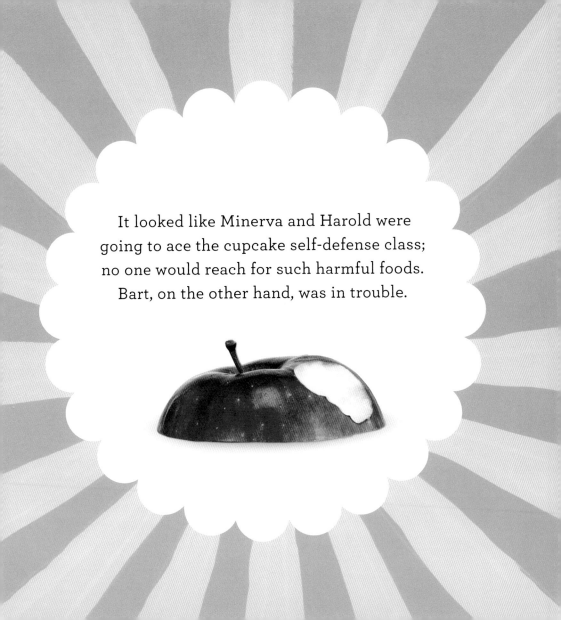

It was another dark, crumby night in Caketropolis. Someone had iced Lenny's partner, and he aimed to figure out why.

ACKNOWLEDGMENTS

While this book may seem like a light and fluffy confection, making it required considerable time and effort from a whole crew (some highly trained professionals and others who were clearly winging it). I'd like to thank my publisher, Lauren Shakely, for spotting the potential in this project, and my editor, Karrie Witkin, for channeling my overall vision. Much credit goes to Danielle Deschenes, for bringing the cupcake world vividly to life with her stunning background artwork and graphic design. Thank you, Megan McLaughlin, for your witty contributions to the set production. Dylan Babb deserves much props for wrangling all of those teeny, tiny props. Alison Watts and Dylan, thank you both for bringing so much enthusiasm and creativity to the task of styling the cupcake cast. Many thanks to Amy Sims, for her patience behind the camera, and Jim Massey, for meticulously directing each shot. Thank you, Kristen Swensson, for doctoring the manuscript. Carole and Josh Jordan, thank you so much for your support and helping hands.

HEY, SWEETIE!